T0102881

The Church and the Kingdom

by

Archbishop Hirron Ignatius Williams
&
Apostle Linda Williams

Order this book online at www.trafford.com
or email orders@trafford.com

Most Trafford titles are also available at major online book retailers.

Print information available on the last page.

ISBN: 978-1-4269-1387-7(sc)

Trafford rev. 07/12/2018

North America & international
toll-free: 1 888 232 4444 (USA & Canada)
fax: 812 355 4082

About The Author

Archbishop Hirron Williams is the presiding prelate & founder of The Cathedral of the Holy Spirit at New Abundant Life Deliverance Ministries in Elba, Alabama. He is the first African-American in the State of Alabama to be consecrated in full vestment as bishop. On August 17, 1997 marked a day in history of Archbishop being the first African-American holding a key to The City of Elba. The legal document filed at Elba's Courthouse records August 17th as "Bishop Hirron Williams Day". He and his wife, Apostle Linda, have graced the New Abundant Life Ministries for 26 years with zeal, wisdom, and prophetic insight. A ministry that God has laid to their charge —

for a people willing to reach their Destiny and Purpose with flowing in the gifts of the spirit and in the supernatural power of God.

After years of faithful service, Archbishop Williams recognized the need for spiritual covering that would provide wisdom, guidance and oversight by request to enrich the development and productivity in the ministry. With the leading of the Lord to seek new direction, he founded The Prophetic Ecumenical Council of Churches International Ministries. This ministry is headquartered in Elba, Alabama.

Archbishop Williams continued to seek upward mobility for his ministry and was embraced by the late Bishop George D. Lee III, Presiding Bishop of Living Word Christian Center in Augusta, GA. In 2006, God favored Archbishop Williams to serve as the present overseer and pastor of Living Word. Through the Apostolic and Prophetic anointing, Archbishop Hirron & Apostle Linda has allowed their purpose-driven mentality to catapult Living Word Ministry to excelling heights.

God has begun a good work in Augusta, GA, through Archbishop Hirron & Apostle Linda to the extension of an outreach ministry entitled the Kaleo Outreach Ministry. This ministry will be the launching pad of great apostles and prophets for the 21st Century. Through in-depth teaching, believers will be impacted with present-day truths to have a greater understanding of God's system of protocol and the distant office of the apostles and prophets.

Archbishop Williams is committed to making a difference in the community and city. He speaks into the lives of politicians and ministers in prison facilities, nursing homes, youth involved in gang activity and to the Body of Believers across the United States of America. Over the past 20 years, Archbishop Williams served as a radio personality every Saturday morning from 8:00 - 10:00 a.m. on WELB 1350 AM radio station in Elba, AL.

In addition, he design to help establish a television ministry for three years on WTVY-4 every Sunday morning 6:00-6:30 entitled, "Charging Destiny through the Prophetic".

Unanimous calls and commendable remarks were served as Archbishop's profound teachings of the Word of God reign in the coverage area. With practical skills and wisdom, Archbishop launched another televised broadcast in DeFuniak Springs, Florida which aired every Monday, Wednesday, and Friday evenings from 5:30 –6:30 p.m. on TV 24.

With diligence and precision, Archbishop authors four books that he feels is very important to the Body of Christ entitled: "Are You Crazy Enough to Believe All You Need is in a Seed?," "Understanding the Prophetic," "Your Destiny is Hid in Another Man," as well as "The Church of 21st Century".

Archbishop is a man with wisdom, grace, class, style and integrity. He is a dreamer - He is a prophet of the Lord.

DEDICATION

I would like to dedicate this book, The Church and The Kingdom to my family, my wife, Apostle Linda, and my children, Lyntresa Shenese, Marissa Omega, Abia Isaiah, and Demetrius Jermaine. My prayer is that this book would be one of the books that would continue to inspire my family to seek after the Kingdom of God and the church of men. That it would inspire other generations of my family to walk under the apostolic and the prophetic anointing that me and their mother walk under. So that not only do we pass down the wisdom in this book but we also pass down the anointing that's on our lives to our children, their children, their children, and their children.

We also pray that this book would be a blessing to you and to your families.

Grace, Peace, and Liberation.

Contents

Chapter one Two Entities 1

Chapter Two Who's Your Daddy? 5

Chapter Three A Form of Godliness 10

Chapter Four Kingdom Power 14

Chapter Five Violent Faith 35

Appendix 47

CHAPTER 1

The church and the kingdom are two different entities. Almost everyone can claim that they have been to church some time in their lives. But how many can say that you've been introduced to the Kingdom of God? You can be a part of the church, but never a part of the kingdom.

Kingdom mentality requires change and most of us are afraid of change. We are scared to come out of our comfort zones and face what you may call the "demons" of change. Jesus made the statement: "repent and be converted for the kingdom of God is at hand."

In other words, it's close to you. Another scripture tells us that the kingdom doesn't come with observation, but the kingdom of God is already within you (Luke 17:20, 21).

It is noteworthy to state that just because you go to church doesn't mean the kingdom of God is within you. That just means you're in the church. We have to understand that God, the ALL POWERFUL, ALL KNOWING GOD wants us to understand the kingdom.

When you think about the kingdom, it's only God's way of doing things. It's God's arrangement of things. IT IS GOD IN ACTION. We have got to understand that we were created for kingdom work. We were created to fulfill destiny and purpose in the earth.

What part does the church play in the Kingdom? The church plays a very important part. Many speak poorly about the church, but I'm not putting the church down, for the church is the VEHICLE TO GET YOU INTO THE KINGDOM.

Without the church you'll be on the outside looking in, wondering: how can I be a part of this kingdom mindset? You know, if you're not in the church, you can't get into the kingdom. Jesus said: I am the way, I am the truth, I am the light (John 14:6).

You must go to church and be a part of some church in order to begin the qualification process to be a part of the kingdom. Many people are just trying to be in church, hoping that would be sufficient. Then there are those who keep going from church to church, saying that they are a part of the kingdom. But the devil is a liar. We have got to understand that God created us to be in His kingdom.

If you are a part of that kingdom, that means you have authority. John 3:1 "There was a man of the Pharisees, named Nicodemus, a ruler of the Jews: the same came to Jesus by night and said unto him, Rabbi (teacher), we know that thou art a teacher come from God, for no man can do these miracles that thou doest, except God be with him."

He began to understand that Jesus was sent from God because of the power that was in his life. Nicodemus, a student of the law, understood the difference he was seeing in the life of Jesus.

Nicodemus understood the rituals that others, like himself performed, but he realized that Jesus was not like any other individual. He saw something in Jesus he did not see in the other religious leaders.

He saw the power - Kingdom Power - resting upon Jesus. You see, you have power when you're part of the kingdom. The church at large today is denying the power of God. They speak about it with their lips, but there is no manifestation. Truth be told, they don't want a powerful manifestation, for they are being led by dumb idols.

CHAPTER 2

I Corinthians 4:15 states: "For though ye have ten thousand instructors in Christ, yet have ye not many fathers." You don't have many that take the time to impart. A father is a protector, life-giver, and provider. You have a lot of preachers that's preaching, but they are not fathers. The word father comes from the greek word "patrikos" which means life-giver, protector, and provider. You have a lot of teachers but you don't have many fathers.

You don't have many that will protect you, provide for you and give you life. That's what we need today. Fathers who are willing to "lay down their lives." That's why when you find a "father" in the kingdom and in the gospel, you need to connect and stay connected. For you have a lot of preachers, but not many fathers.

Consider this: have you found your father yet? Have you found your connection? If you have found that father, then he is the one who imparts unto you. He is the one from whom you get your identity. Messages like "who's your daddy" really bring home the message that fatherhood is important in the Body of Christ. This may even be compared to your earthly father. How many of you would have loved to have a father who protected you, provided for you, and whom you proudly identified as yours.

Just as fathers are seemingly absent in the natural, so we find that true fathers in the gospel are rare. So encourage the fathers in the faith. Demonstrate your appreciation. Let them see in the here and now that their labor has not been in vain.

You know Jesus identified the scribes and the Pharisees. He said: "you're of your father the devil" (John 8:44).

In other words, the way you're acting, your actions depict those of your daddy. Your daddy is not the father – God the father, but it's the other person.

So when a person is acting out the wrong thing, guess who is their daddy? Of course. The devil. Who's your daddy? Every time you move, and every time you breathe, you're been given a paternity test to find out who's your daddy. Who are you acting like? Am I acting like daddy God or am I acting like the devil?

If you are part of the kingdom, there are certain things that will be manifested in your life. When they are not manifested, many times it is out of ignorance. I Corinthians 4:15-16 ....for in Christ Jesus I have begotten you through the gospel. Wherefore I beseech (beg) you, be ye followers of me. Paul wasn't afraid to tell the people when you're part of the kingdom, follow me.

If you are headed in the right direction to the right place, there's no reason to tell people to pray about it. No, you don't have to pray about it. You follow the man of God. Verse 17 states:

For this cause have I sent unto you Timotheus, who is my beloved son. Paul is saying, look, here is one serving faithfully. Here is one that is my son. In other words, he's just like me. … faithful in the Lord who shall bring you into remembrance of my ways…

That is the reason every leader ought to be reminding the rest of the saints of Almighty God what the father of the house has said. Everyone should be echoing the voice of the "father."

The bible said we ought to speak the same thing (I.Cor.1:10).

The leaders of the house should be saying the same thing. Two things leaders should understand snakes in the church and the kingdom. Verse 17-19 … who shall bring you into the remembrance of my ways in Christ, as I teach everywhere in every church. He was teaching about the kingdom. Now some are puffed up as though I would not come to you. But I will come to you shortly, if the Lord will, and will know not the speech of them which are puffed up, but the power.

The word says he's not coming to you with speech puffed up; to paraphrase, he's not coming to you with enticing words, but he's coming to you with power. There's the difference. Many people know how to do everything and articulate it just right, yet have no power. That is the reason the bible says that some people have a form of godliness but deny the power.

CHAPTER 3

We need to have power. Joshua and the children of Israel had power in their shout. When they shouted, the walls came down. We have a lot of people shouting without any power. We must manifest the power. The way we manifest the power is by living right and by standing on the Word.

You can't have any power away from the word for the Word – Jesus is power. We must then realize that God has not called us just to be a part of the church, but to be a part of the kingdom. The Church of the 21st century is not the church of the Apostles of old.

The word church comes from the word ecclesia which means the called out ones –

and in today's church, there's hardly anybody that's called out. Everything goes. There's no separation. If we've been called out then we shouldn't be acting like everyone else.

We should be different. Have we become so much like the world that the line between the church and the world has become blurred and is now blended? Brethren, that should not be. We shouldn't act like everyone else is acting. We shouldn't talk like everyone else is talking. If we're part of the kingdom, we cannot operate like everyone else. We have to operate with POWER. It's time for folks to feel the power.

That's the reason people are not getting healed in the church, because people don't want to manifest power. We're so concerned with numbers – quantity and not quality.

Why would you want a thousand powerless people? We have to tap into the power of Almighty God. WE NEED HIS POWER.

Paul emphasized he was not coming all puffed up, he was not coming to you trying to talk like everyone else. He was not trying to act like everyone else. He was coming with power. Now is not the time to display exegetics or demonstrate homiletics. Now is the time to manifest power. We don't need the art of preaching, nor scripture commentaries. WE NEED POWER.

People are concerned about family members hooked on drugs. Others are so sick that they don't know what to do. We need to see the power of God in manifestation.

When you are in the kingdom, the power of God must be manifested. And I'm persuaded by the Holy Ghost that people in the church today manifest a religious power. Instead of saying the church is my vehicle to the kingdom, or the church is the doorway to the kingdom, they have become complacent and accept religion as the norm.

But in order to be a part of the kingdom I must get into the right church. Being in the right church exposes you to the kingdom. That's the reason the bible says seek ye first the kingdom of God. He didn't say seek ye first the church. He said seek ye first the kingdom.

That is Gods' way of doing things. I must first find out:

How would God handle this or how would God do this? Knowing how Rev.Jack Rabbit wants it done is no concern of mine. Hearing what Sis. Cornbread has to say is good, and she may have a lot to say, but it must line up with what God is saying. Ultimately, I really need to see how does God want me to deal with this situation?

Once you seek the kingdom, you have nothing about which to worry. For everything else will be added unto you (Matt.6:33). Those things will be seeking after you. You'll have the universe lining up behind you demanding that everything you need come to you. Hallelujah! But you have to hold on to the kingdom. However, if you don't seek the kingdom, you will be seeking after things.

CHAPTER 4

When you begin to think about the kingdom, you think about what king is ruling over the dome, the dimension in which you are, because anytime there is a kingdom, there has to be a king. It is no wonder that Jesus declared that he was King of kings. He was not only king, but he was king over all kings.

We therefore need to understand that we are part of a powerful kingdom. It's not weak. There may be weak people around, but those who are walking in the kingdom are not weak individuals.

I Corinthians 4:20 says for the kingdom of God in not in word.... It's not in what you say, because people will fool you and make you think that they are in the kingdom. They'll act just like that half frozen snake acted around the Apostle Paul.

It will make you think it's a stick. In reality, the snake was just waiting for it to get hot, because snakes only come out when it gets hot. Verse 20 reads: For the kingdom of God is not in word, but in power. We are supposed to be seeking after the kingdom. People want to be a part of everything but the kingdom. For example, any organization that's around today, people are trying their best to be a part of that organization.

What about the kingdom of God? I believe we ought to be a part of the kingdom. Once you're a part of the kingdom, you're subject to the king.

To whom are you subject? To whom are you submitted? When you are submitted to the king, you should never have to worry about anything, because in a democratic society, people worry about taking care of themselves. However, when you are part of a kingdom, you are the kings' responsibility, thereby relieving you of any worry. Because I'm his responsibility, everything that I need he's going to supply, for he has already said when you're part of the kingdom, he knows your need before you even ask him. Phillipians 4:19 says it like this: But my God shall supply all your need according to his riches in glory by Christ Jesus.

We are God's responsibility if we are submitted to the king. Your responsibility is to submit to the king and be in the kingdom. Let me make this quite clear - I'm not talking about the church. I'm talking about being in the kingdom.

Being in church does not make you a part of the kingdom. We now have a lot of people who'll be quick to tell you: I'm a Christian. I go to church. That's the reason I don't call myself a Christian. I call myself a kingdom man.

Jesus wasn't a Christian. He was a kingdom man and operated on kingdom principles. That is why everything he did, he did because he had all authority and power in his hands. He knew things couldn't deny him. Why? Because everything that's in this realm was subject to him. Glory to God!

Romans 14 verse 17: For the kingdom of God is not meat and drink. To what was Paul referring? The Kingdom of God is not what I eat and drink. The Apostle Paul was been accused by the church. The church was saying that Paul was eating meat that was offered up to idols. When they went and offered up meat to idols, Paul, being hungry, would eat some of the meat.

He didn't care to whom it was offered, so the people began to accuse him. Religious people will accuse you. Paul was in good company. They accused Jesus. When you begin to find out who you are and whose you are, people won't like you very much.

Your walk is doing the talking. Your lifestyle is letting them know that the game is over. Everyone now sees that what you claimed to possess is nonexistent.

He's out there living the life he's supposed to live, preaching the gospel he's supposed to preach and then the religious one of the day tried to find something that they could expose. So they pounced on him eating meat that was offered up to idols.

Didn't the scribes and Pharisees do the same thing to Jesus? Paul is letting them know that the kingdom of God is not meat and drink. In other words, he did not care to whom it was offered. He knew that he had power over any idol, and was not afraid. Romans 14:17 continues... but righteousness, and peace, and joy in the Holy Ghost. When you're in the kingdom, you're in right standing and peace. If you don't have peace, one way is to get into the kingdom.

Are you in the kingdom? Why not give yourself a kingdom test?

1. ARE YOU IN RIGHT STANDING WITH GOD?

2. DO YOU HAVE ANY PEACE?

If you know you're in right standing with God, that's beginning to say that you are part of the kingdom. However, if you don't have any right standing with God and you never have any peace, you need to check yourself. YOU MAY NOT BE A PART OF THE KINGDOM.

The bible says: Examine yourselves, whether ye be in the faith (II Corinthians 13:5). Therefore, every now and then it is necessary to do self examination to find out whether you are still in the place you were yesterday. If you are not in that place, that place of yesterday, you are a backslider. If you are not going forward, you're going backward.

Examine yourself. If you're always sad, you are not a part of the kingdom. If you are always looking "rough," and complaining, you're not a part of the kingdom.

When you're a part of the kingdom, it comes with righteousness, it comes with peace and it comes with joy in the Holy Ghost. Joy is different from happiness. Happiness comes from a word which means something must happen to you first. But when you have joy, joy comes out of the Holy Ghost. That is one thing that is birthed out of the Holy Ghost: joy.

And the bible says if you have no joy, begin to leap for it (Luke 6:23).

When you examine that word joy, you'll find that it means you can jump up and down, and you can rejoice. It also means you can turn in a circle violently or you can dance before the Lord. So as you dance before the Lord, as you turn in a circle violently, and as you leap up and down, God begins to give you joy.

When no joy is in my life, I must act out the word: that is, I must leap for it. Regardless of how you may be feeling right now, you've got to stretch and do what the Word says. When we do so, when we show the Lord that we are willing to stand on the Word, then yes, joy comes. Joy comes to your heart, joy comes to your soul. Joy comes. And when joy comes, joy unspeakable and full of glory, then you know you are in the kingdom.

You have completed your self examination. You have righteousness, you are in right standing with God, you have peace, and now hallelujah, you have joy. That is the foundation of the kingdom. Don't allow anybody to convince you otherwise.

When you are seeking the kingdom, you want to be certain that you are in right standing with God. You want to be honest with Him And let Him know that "God, I want to be right with You. I want to be in that place with you God, for I know that as I seek the kingdom, peace is coming to me because I need your peace God. God, with all this stuff around me, I need some peace in the midst of all this confusion. I'm seeking your kingdom." And because He's a loving God, peace comes.

After you find peace, then all of a sudden joy comes, for joy comes right out of peace. Now listen married women, if you listen to your man, the only thing he cries out for is peace. Don't distract him when he's seeking the kingdom. Encourage him to seek the kingdom.

Do whatever it takes to get your man peace. Find something for the children to do or somewhere for them to go, for the priest of the household needs to seek the kingdom.

St. John 3:2 again reads: The same came to Jesus by night, and said unto him, Rabbi, we know that thou art a teacher come from God – we know from where you come. We hear and know what you are teaching.

Do you really know what he's teaching? If you don't have a revelation of your teacher, your mentor, you'll never be given the keys to the kingdom. Do you know your teacher? Do you know your mentor? Do you have a mentor? Everybody says: I have the keys but if you haven't received a revelation of the one that's over you, you are deceiving yourself.

Continuing with verse 2: "for no man can do these miracles that thou doest, except God be with him." This work is not being done by the power of man. This is being done by the power of God. In other words, we see something in you that we don't see in everybody else.

Remember, Nicodemus sat on the Sanhedrin council as one who dissected the law. His circumstances forced him to approach Jesus by night, seeing that he was at work during the day. Being a religious man, he was in the temple discussing the law with men just like him.

However, on his own time, he chose to see Jesus. Then he began to acknowledge what he saw in the life of Jesus. When you're in the kingdom, people cannot deny the power that's in your life. They may say lot of "low down" things about you, but they cannot deny the power that is being manifested in your life.

Verse three states: Verily, verily I say unto thee, except a man be born again, he cannot see the kingdom of God. In actuality he was saying, except a man is changed in his thinking, unless a man is changed in his mind, he cannot see the kingdom of God.

For example, the only way you became saved is that first, you had a change of mind. One old song said: "I went to a meeting one night, my heart wasn't right and something got a hold of me…" When that something "got a hold" you had to change your mind. Therefore Jesus is telling Nicodemus that he has to change his mind. He must change the way he's been seeing things. If you do not, you cannot see the kingdom of God.

In order to understand this, we, like Nicodemus, must be changed in our minds. But we as the Ecclesia, the church, call it being born again or being saved. We need to have a shifting in our thinking. If you don't believe me, look around in your life and the church at large. Are you pleased with what you see? Most of us will not be pleased. That is clear evidence that we do need to make a mental shift.

As soon as you begin to make that shift in your thinking, suddenly peace enters. So if you change the way you think, you change everything that happens in your life. Jesus was telling Nicodemus, "you're religious. You know what the Word says, but you can't see anything. You can't see the kingdom because you have not had a born again experience."

Lots of people know the word but are not born again. The word born again also means to be born from above. So if you were born from above, you would be thinking at a higher level. Another song used to say: "elevate your mind, let's go higher." When we are born again, we can elevate our minds. Once our minds are elevated, then we can go higher.

Because the mind and body is connected, wherever your mind is, your body ultimately will be in that same place. Nicodemus must be born again before he can see the kingdom. The principle is the same. In order for you and I to see the kingdom of God, we must be born again. This implies that some things cannot be seen unless you have been born again.

Millions of people attend church. However that is not the criteria. You must have a personal experience with Jesus. In order for your mind to be transformed, or in order for your mind to be changed, an experience with Jesus is mandatory. No experience, no transformation. No transformation equals lack of vision concerning the kingdom.

Nicodemus begins to allow his religious nature to surface. He asks: how can a man be born when he is old? Can he enter the second time in his mother's womb and be born? Nicodemus knows in the natural, that's impossible. Yet he asks the question.

Religious people will get into a silly mode at times. A silliness is coming forth out of him right now for he is saying "I don't understand."

Even though Jesus told him that in order to see the kingdom of God, he must be born again, he still asked that question. That question also showed his desire and his hunger. Even though his talking is a little off, he's still demonstrating hunger. Blessed are they that hunger and thirst after righteousness, for they shall be filled. Or they shall be made complete (Matt.5:6). So if you're hungering and thirsting after righteousness, you will be made complete for you are seeking after the right thing. What are you seeking?

Jesus did not ignore Nicodemus' question. He answered: Verily, verily, I say unto thee, except a man be born of water and of the Spirit, he cannot enter into the kingdom of God. Man has to be born of water and of the Spirit.

Many times people don't believe it, but that's

the reason we still practice baptism. We have to be born of the water and we have to be born of the Spirit. We must have at least two baptisms. One is the baptism of water and the other is the baptism in fire. If you have not been baptized in the fire of the Holy Ghost, then you've just been filled. And if you've been filled, then the need exists for you to be filled again.

But if you've been baptized, submerged, the fire of God dwells on the inside of you. Have you been submerged into the kingdom? Have you been submerged into the Spirit of God or have done like that old commercial… "a lil dab will do."?

People in the church many times have the same mindset as that commercial. All they want is a quick fix, "a lil dab," and then go right on their way. If you don't give them what they want, they will still go. People want to dictate to the man and woman of God, and when they don't respond as others think they should, they leave or threaten to leave. They'll say I need to move somewhere else. By whose authority are challenging the "set man"?

Jesus was trying to get Nicodemus to understand – you must have a born again experience in order to get into the kingdom of God. You cannot enter the kingdom without a changed mind. You cannot embrace the power of the kingdom until you meet the requirement: a changed mind – a born again experience.

So if you are born again, you can embrace the kingdom fully. Not only can you see it, but you can enter into it. In other words, you can interact with what's going on in the kingdom.

In other countries around the world, the government is set up in a kingdom format. They physically have a king or queen and operate very differently from our system of government. The word says that the kingdoms of this world have become the kingdom of our gods.(Rev. 11:15) People always talk about the end of the world. However, the bible never said the end of the world. It talks about the end of the age.

When the end of the age takes place, it's the end of the arrangement of the worldly kingdom. Then God will set up his kingdom in the earth and we will rule in the kingdom. Hallelujah!

That's the reason when we come to church, when we assemble, we should be practicing to rule in the kingdom.

Jesus is still responding to Nicodemus: That which is born of the flesh is flesh and that which is born of the Spirit is Spirit. Marvel not that I say unto thee, ye must be born again. Jesus let him know – don't stand here in amazement looking at me! Nicodemus was probably looking at him with his mouth open trying to understand what the Lord had just said. Knowing that Nicodemus was a religious man, he was trying to understand how Jesus answer covered his question. What he did not realize, Jesus was speaking to him on a higher level.

When people are really hooked into the kingdom, they don't talk like regular church folks. Regular church folks complain, swear they have no complaints, but are quick to say "the lord said".

I Corinthians 12:1 -2 read: "Now concerning spiritual gifts, brethren, I would not have you ignorant. Ye know that ye were Gentiles, carried away unto these dumb idols, even as ye were led." Apostle Paul did not want you to be ignorant concerning spiritual gifts. You know that you were unsaved people carried away unto these dumb idols.

What is a dumb idol? A dumb idol is anything that's absent from the voice and presence of God. Anything that does not have the voice of God speaking through it or the presence of God with it is a dumb idol.

That's the reason you can't just go to any church because the voice and presence of God is absent in some churches. Without His presence, then it's nothing but a dumb idol leading the people.

Many can pretend they are not dumb idols. However when it becomes obvious that there's nothing godly coming from them, no "word" coming out of them, you have to conclude that indeed dumb idols are leading them. There are lots of scriptures that people quote. Drunks also quote scriptures. As a matter of fact, they'll preach a message about hell to you, knowing they're "tanked up", but they'll talk scripture to you. Should you then follow them just because they quoted scriptures?

Paul said brethren, I don't want you to be ignorant concerning spiritual gifts. Verse 2 says you were carried away unto these dumb idols. In other words, you were overzealous running behind dumb stuff. Be careful what you allow to become attached to you for that can drain you of the energy you ought to be using for spreading the gospel. Don't allow yourself to be caught up in the gimmicks people use to separate you from your money all in the name of religion.

Why is it people can be carried away quicker with "dumb stuff" than they can with the right stuff? In other words, how can people accept as truth something that's obviously flawed but refuse to accept the truth?

When people run after quick fixes, that's a sure way of knowing that they are not seeking the kingdom. Instead, you must go through the process in order to receive what God has for you. There is no short cut. When you are going through the process, you are in essence (doing) participating in a qualifying run.

In the racing world, you must race that car around the track in order to qualify for the big race. So it is with God. When you are going through the process, it's qualifying you for the blessings of God. No process? No blessings. It's as simple as that. But if you go through the process, you can have the blessings of God. Amen! So I must go through the process before I do anything else.

Jesus had to go through the process. As Jesus was being made ready to be crucified, the bible said that as he was coming into the city, there was a crowd of people. Some were in front of him and some were behind him. The crowd was bursting with excitement. Here comes the King of the Jews. To honor him, they began to take off their garments and lay them on the ground. After they couldn't lay any more garments on the ground, they began to lay palm leaves.

Don't you remember when Johnathan and David shared each other's clothes? They cut covenant one with the other. Johnathan took off his robe and gave it to David. He also took his sword and gave it to him. He declared that their hearts were knitted together.

In like manner the people were knitting their hearts together with Jesus as they laid the palm leaves down culminating it with HOSANNA, HOSANNA, HOSANNA to the king. When last have you cried out hosanna? When last have you laid palms down? You may be saying, I can't lay any palms down! You're wrong! We need to lay our palms down in prayer.

When we are talking to the Lord, we need to be talking to Him with our palms lifted up! Hallelujah! Every now and then throw them up in the face of the Lord! Magnify Him! Glorify Him! Demonstrate your thankfulness to Him! For our God is truly worthy to be praised, our God is truly worthy to be worshipped! Glory to God! If Jesus was not crucified, you and I would not have any right to the kingdom! But glory to God, He bore our sins in His body on the tree, giving us access into the kingdom!

He had to go through the process - the process set aside - to bring us into the kingdom. So when you go through the process, that's your key to bring you into your divinely appointed place. No one but you can keep you from entering into that place. That place brings you into divine connection. It brings you into divine destiny. YOU MUST GO THROUGH THE PROCESS! Jesus told Nicodemus there's no way around it. It's a process.

CHAPTER 5

In order for you to see the kingdom, in order for you to enter the kingdom, you have to change some things. You have to change some things in your dome – your head. Consider this: if your head is your dome, who is ruling? Who is king in your dome? Who is king in your thought patterns? Who is king in your decision making? Who is king sitting on the throne of you as an individual? Who have you allowed to be king?

Have you allowed the system or the kingdom of this world to control you? Are you moving just like the world? Are you operating using the world's system? Are you scared like the world?

That's the reason this country is always

talking about terrorists because they want this country cling to fear so that they could rule and reign as they desire. But when you're part of the kingdom, there's no fear in the kingdom of God. God did not give us a spirit of fear, but He gave us a spirit of love, power and a soundness of mind. When you are in the kingdom, you have a sound mind. Declare to yourself that you have a sound mind.

II Timothy 4 verses 1-2 reads: "I charge thee therefore before God, and the Lord Jesus Christ who shall judge the quick and the dead at his appearing and his kingdom; preach the word..."

Kingdom people are concerned about preaching the word. Not just any word, but a pure word, a present day truth, not just a yesterday's truth. Why must we preach a present day truth? Our God is a progressive God and he has a progressive people.

If you are still hanging around the waters of past experience, you will never have a true experience with God. It is good talk about what he's done yesterday, but you cannot live in the smoke of yesterday. You have to live in the fire of today! Amen! Glory to God!

God is bringing forth and raising up a people now that is strong in the prophetic and apostolic power. These are bold prophets and apostles.

The word also says: "be instant in season, out of season; reprove, rebuke, exhort with all longsuffering and doctrine. For the time will come when they will not endure sound doctrine." I believe we're in that time right now. Everybody ought to be preaching about the kingdom, for the time will come when people will not endure sound doctrine.

Sound doctrine is nothing but right teaching. They won't want to hear right teaching. They want to hear it mixed with something that will want to make the flesh feel good. The truth does not feel good to the flesh. The truth barbecues the flesh.

Do you remember when the angel in the book of Revelation told him to eat the book? When John ate the book, he said it was sweet to his mouth, but bitter to his belly. What John was actually saying was that to his spirit this was sweet, but to his flesh this was very bitter.

When truth comes forth, it is designed to turn you when you don't want to be turned. That can become quite uncomfortable and irritating. People say that they want the truth. The reality is that most people don't want to hear the truth. They want to hear something that will make them feel good. They want to believe that they are on the right track and no adjustment is needed.

However the word says that the time will come when people will not endure sound doctrine. When you think of the word sound, sound is what you hear.

It also refers to something being steady. For example, when you sit in a chair, you want it to be sound or steady. You want it to be able to support you. Just like that, you should want the word of Almighty God to support and keep you steady.

When the waves of life are taking you up and down and all around, you want the word of the Lord to be an anchor to hold you steady. Distractions come to get you away from the kingdom. How can you say that? With distractions comes another thought pattern. It comes to break your focus. Don't allow anything to break your focus.

With broken focus you are vulnerable to the enemy. II Timothy continues: they will not endure sound doctrine, but after their own lusts shall they heap to themselves teachers, having itching ears. With broken focus, when you are not seeking the kingdom, you'll find people running after teachers who will tell them what they want to hear.

Instead of running after truth, they are running after something unsound. They have itching ears. They don't care if Rev. "Bobo is homosexual. They don't care if he's a child molester. All they know is "I have an itching ear and he is going to tell me what I want to hear."

Since he isn't changed, I know he's not going to try to change me. You must watch yourself if you have an itching ear. You'll do anything to relieve the itch, just as you do in the natural when your ears are itching.

Many people in the spirit realm have busted eardrums. They cannot hear the truth and must be healed in order to hear truth. They have allowed everybody to put something in their ears. They need help! If they do not receive help they will surely do what the word says: they shall turn their ears from the truth and shall be turned unto fables.

It's a dangerous thing to allow "stuff" to scratch your ears for a long time because it ultimately turns you away from the truth. Sadly, these people who turn away from the truth had to have known the truth at some point.

We as the church have become satisfied with those who tickle our ears – tell us what we want to hear. But complacency must be demolished. You must no longer be satisfied with two songs, a poem, and a three point sermon. We must all hunger after truth.

The church of today must grow up. We must go beyond singing nursery rhyme songs such as "this little light of mine". It sounds good, but what about the message? Wouldn't you rather be a doer of the Word? Jesus says: "ye are the light of the world".

The world cannot see you until you're lit up. What good would a 16 watt bulb do in a world of darkness? The church must turn once more to being the light of the world instead of turning to fables.

II Timothy 4:4 reads: and they shall turn away their ears from the truth, and shall be turned unto fables. The church of the twenty first century is turning to fables. Let's look at the fables surrounding Easter. What does easter bunnies have to do with Jesus and his resurrection?

Yet Easter, the Babylonian goddess of fertility is all wrapped up in the Easter celebration. You have religious people that will justify it like this: "the shell of the egg represent the tomb of Jesus. The white part represents the linen in which Jesus was wrapped and the yellow yolk represents Jesus."

Let's tell the truth and stay away from fables. What is the truth? Jesus Christ was crucified. He hung there, bled and died. Then He was buried and resurrected. Hallelujah! Glory to God!

Why give some of his power to an easter bunny? When we're a part of the kingdom, we understand the resurrection and the power of Almighty God. Can I tell you something? Santa Claus is also a lie.

Don't let anybody dictate to you when you should do something for your loved ones. Always remember, it's not about what man sees on the outside, but it's about what God sees when he looks on the heart. Amen. Glory to God. When the heart is right, everything else is right.

Keep away from fables. Verse 5 reads: "but watch thou in all things, endure afflictions... You are going to go through some things because of the truth. When you begin to stand for the truth, many of your "friends" will disappear. Keep speaking the truth and you'll notice many won't clamor for your presence.

If you want to get some people out of your life, change the way you think. As you change the way you've been thinking and seeing, they will make a sound flying out of your life.

The verse continues: do the work of an evangelist, make full proof of thy ministry.

Begin to stir up people. Everyone in the pews must be doing something. What's that? Spread the truth! Be excited about Jesus. Don't take a back seat. Interject Jesus in every conversation. If it had not been for Jesus, where would you be today? Don't be intimidated by skeptics. Stir people up with the truth. I Timothy 4:6 says: For I am now ready to be offered, and the time of my departure is at hand.

This is a father talking to his son. He understood that he would soon be leaving. But he was engrossed in encouraging his son in the gospel. It is time to learn how to encourage those all around us. Look past the titles, positions, the outward appearance and see as Jesus sees – precious lives that he would die for again.

We are all special to Jesus, so we should be

"special," "compassionate," and "loving" one to another. We have to learn how to speak a word. One of my prayers is: God give me a word in season for them that are weary. I need something for them who are about to give up and quit. I need a word that would pull a hopeless person out of a hopeless situation and give them some hope.

In order to have a word we must be a part of the kingdom. Matthew 11:12 reads: And from the days of John the Baptist until now, the kingdom of heaven suffereth violence, and the violent take it by force. Can I tell you something? Violence here is referring to the people of God becoming violent in the spirit. No more playing church. It's time for a life change.

When you hear people complaining in the grocery store or on the job, you let God give you a word that will halt the complaints. Whether it's about the price of food, gas, sickness, trouble with the kids or whatever, let the word of the Lord flow through you bringing a change in that individual's life. That's the violent taking it by force.

You know there are some things that the enemy tries to deny those who are walking in the kingdom. But the bible says that when a thief is caught, he must restore seven fold. Recognize the thief in your life and demand that he restores as the bible declares. When you are part of the kingdom you begin to recognize what's been taken from you and you put a stop to it.

You don't have to wait for sister cornbread or anyone to agree with you in prayer. You start praying yourself. You let the enemy know that you're going to take it by force because (1) you are in the kingdom and (2) you know it is rightfully yours.

Declare to the enemy to take their hands off because what's for you is for you and there's nothing he or she can do about it. Whatever is yours, declare it now. Take it. Bring it from the spiritual realm into the natural realm. Whether it's an airplane, a house, peace of mind, whatever it is, when you're part of the kingdom, you can decree a thing and it shall be established. Why? We have power because the kingdom comes with power. Declare that you have the power. Every devil is subject to you because you are walking in the kingdom and have power. Your days of fear are over because you have the power. DECLARE IT UNTIL IT BECOMES REALITY.

When you have power signs follow you. Bless God for his power. Bless God for being in the kingdom. Bless God forevermore. Without his selfless act of giving up his only begotten son, we would not be able to declare kingdom power. Now we can boldly say: Jesus, King of Kings and Lord of Lords was crucified for me so that I can walk in kingdom power. Hallelujah! Glory to God! Thank you Lord for a kingdom mindset. Thank you Lord for the power! Declare to yourself: I GOT THE POWER!

APPENDIX

SNAKES IN THE CHURCH

Snakes in the church and snakes in the natural have one thing in common: venom. They will inject poison into you. Although natural snakes are not all poisonous, they are crafty. Whether it is venom to paralyze your body or venom to paralyze your mind, the intent is the same. They want to"take you out".

In Genesis 3 we see the serpent talking to Eve. It seems like a harmless conversation, but we should not become complacent when snakes are around. They are just looking for the opportunity to pounce. So are snakes in the church. These are people who are waiting for the door to be opened so that they can infiltrate your mind with lies. How do you recognize them? Weak people look for other weak people. Infected people always look for other infected people. Sick people always look for other sick people. Remember a serpent's poison is in its head and releases it through its mouth. So when people are going to others with the intent of getting them upset or off focus, mark that person.

Just because someone calls themselves a christian or say they're born again does not mean that they have your best interest at heart. Didn't the Word say… try the spirits whether they are of God…? (I John 4:1) Watch those who are slipping around you trying to poison your mind against what you know to be truth. Ask yourself the question: snake or saint? How does their characteristic line up?

You know the characteristic of a saint and you know the characteristic of a snake. Are they coming to you in a friendly manner but their words cause you to be on guard? Are they demonstrating love? Are they approaching you in attack mode? Snakes in the church.

In verse 4 we see the serpent introducing

rebellion and disloyalty to Eve. Satan in the form of a serpent is telling her that she shall not surely die although God specifically said: "in the day that thou eatest thereof thou shalt surely die."(Genesis 2:17)

Don't allow someone to use the word Christian and think that you ought to give ear to what they are saying. Would you allow just anyone in your home? How about dumping trash into your home? Of course not! By the same token, don't allow anyone to speak just anything in your ear for you (your entire body) are the temple of the Holy Ghost.

Printed in the United States
By Bookmasters